a guide to

CORNWALL

by

WEEKEND JOURNALS

WORDS
Milly Kenny-Ryder

DESIGN
Simon Lovell

PHOTOGRAPHY
Gabriel Kenny-Ryder

weekendjournals.co.uk

CONTENTS

—

Our chosen places take you on a journey
travelling around the Cornish coast.

Preface	9
Map of Cornwall	12
TRE, POL & PEN	14
COOMBESHEAD FARM	16
TEMPLE	18
KUDHVA	20
ST TUDY INN	22
RESTAURANT NATHAN OUTLAW	24
CARN MAR	26
SURFSIDE	28
PAUL AINSWORTH AT NO. 6	30
TREVIBBAN MILL	32
THE SCARLET	34
PAVILION	36
WATERGATE BAY HOTEL	38
NANCARROW	40
DOR & TAN	42
TATE ST IVES	44
TREVOSE HARBOUR HOUSE	46
BARBARA HEPWORTH MUSEUM AND SCULPTURE GARDEN	48
SANDS & SAMPHIRE STUDIOS	52
PLUMBLINE	54
PORT OF CALL	56
THE OLD CUSTOM HOUSE	58

ANIMA MUNDI   60

YALLAH COFFEE KIOSK   62

LEACH POTTERY   64

THE GURNARD'S HEAD   66

THE MINACK THEATRE   68

LOVETTS   70

ARTIST RESIDENCE   72

NO. 56   74

CHAPEL HOUSE   76

TOTTI   80

JUBILEE POOL   82

TREMENHEERE SCULPTURE GARDENS   86

NEW YARD   88

POTAGER GARDEN   90

THE SANDY DUCK   92

TORO   94

ESPRESSINI   96

BOTANICAL ATELIER   98

BEACON COFFEE   100

THE SEAFOOD BAR   102

THE WAREHOUSE, ORIGIN COFFEE ROASTERS   104

THE HIDDEN HUT   106

FITZROY   108

ISLES OF SCILLY   110

An Interview with Simon Stallard   114

An Interview with Darren Little   118

Further Ideas   122

PREFACE

—

There's something special about Cornwall. Perhaps it's the light, the blissful isolation, the evidence of a mysterious past or just the dramatic coastline. We have spent years exploring this enchanted county, meeting lots of the locals and becoming attuned to their slower pace of life. The shops have eccentric opening times based around the tides and the surf, and the restaurant kitchens close when the daily catch has all gone - it feels refreshing and healthy to live this way.

There are many celebrated places to visit time and time again in Cornwall, and I know frequent visitors often have a favourite haunt or ritual - a beach or an ice-cream shop they eagerly return to every trip. For us, it is the magical cloutie tree at Madron Wishing Well or enjoying a pasty from Philps after a bracing dip in the sea.

Although much of Cornwall's appeal is nostalgic, there are innovators who are bringing modern, stylish but sympathetic ideas to the Cornish scene: boutique hotels for hip travellers, gastronomic eateries for keen foodies and contemporary galleries and gardens to satisfy discerning aesthetes. Hopefully you will be encouraged to venture further afield to the exciting and special venues we have discovered, sometimes in the most unlikely corners.

There is so much more to experience in Cornwall than initially meets the eye, and I hope this book will inspire you to see and do more while visiting.

Milly Kenny-Ryder

MAP OF CORNWALL

—

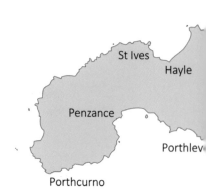

St Ives

Hayle

Penzance

Porthlev

Porthcurno

Isles of Scilly

Bude

Tintagel

Launceston

Port Isaac

Polzeath

Padstow

Bodmin

Newquay

St Austell

Looe

St Agnes

Fowey

Truro

Penryn

Portscatho

Falmouth

St Mawes

Helston

TRE, POL & PEN

—

Farm Shop & Café

Lezant, Launceston, PL15 9NN
01566 706 527
trepolandpen.co.uk

It is the rich and plentiful produce in Cornwall that has helped make this county such an alluring foodie destination. From Launceston to Land's End there are artisan producers forging the way with craft beer and wine, exciting sustainable farming projects and all kinds of other speciality food and produce.

Tre, Pol & Pen is an encyclopedic farm shop, offering the very best Cornish ingredients, ideal for a shopping trip before heading home or to a self-catering cottage. Located on the family farm, just over the Devon-Cornwall border, this expansive shop and kitchen opened in 2019. Highlights include their own Red Ruby beef from the surrounding fields, seasonal fruit and vegetables from the Tamar valley and homeware from local makers.

Their airy café serves wholesome food throughout the day as well as hosting crowd-pleasing pizza nights, making use of their stone-bake oven.

COOMBESHEAD FARM

—

Guesthouse & Restaurant

Lewannick, Launceston, PL15 7QQ
01566 782 009
coombesheadfarm.co.uk

Just five minutes' drive from the Devon-Cornwall border, Coombeshead Farm has everything you need for a weekend break. Founded by Pitt Cue Co-owner Tom Adams and Michelin-starred chef April Bloomfield, it is a foodie destination with beautiful bedrooms as a bonus. Set amongst sixty-six acres of meadows and woodland, this restaurant, guesthouse, working farm and bakery has a peaceful atmosphere that encourages you to feel at home.

The Georgian farmhouse has been designed by Ali Childs, of Studio Alexandra, who has thoughtfully juxtaposed rustic and retro countryside memorabilia with modern features and luxurious amenities.

Dinner is a highlight, served in the renovated barn restaurant. The menu features produce from the farm used in an innovative way, naturally emphasising the essence of the area. Dinner and Sunday lunch are available to non-residents as well as staying guests.

The onsite bakery uses British stone ground flour to bake sourdough loaves and offers regular bread making workshops.

TEMPLE

—

Restaurant & Shop

10 Granville Terrace, Bude, EX23 8JZ
01288 354 739
templecornwall.com

Temple is a neighbourhood restaurant and store in the North Cornwall town of Bude. This colourful space opened in late 2017, a calming place to sit and relax while enjoying good food and organic wines.

Run by a team of four creatives, this innovative venue is a celebration of design and culture. The small boutique stocks a range of carefully curated lifestyle goods and independent clothing brands.

The restaurant features bold flavours and fresh, wholesome ingredients, from brunch through to intimate dinners. The team focus on using seasonal produce, working with local farmers and helping to make a positive impact on the surrounding environment. Coffee is made with Allpress beans and vibrant juices provide a health kick. In the evenings they introduce a sharing based ethos and regularly invite guest chefs to take part in their 'Temple Takeover' residencies.

Our menus change frequently to reflect our constant search for new flavours & local producers

Our clothing & homeware goods are curated with a devotion to superior quality & design

Our coffee is from Alpress. They use a unique hot air roasting technique which gives it a splendid taste & they are also just really bloody nice people

Our sourdough is baked by Ben Glazer at Coombeshead Farm. (equally very nice people)

We use selected cuts of meat from organic & high welfare farms

Every bottle of wine we have selected for Temple is from a certified organic producer

We love what we do, we thank you for supporting us

- TEMPLE TEAM

KUDHVA

—

Cabins & Camping

Sanding Road, Trebarwith Strand, Tintagel, PL34 0HH
kudhva.com

Cornwall is full of hidden gems and surprising ventures, if you are willing to search for them. Kudhva is a wild and magical escape in the Tintagel countryside. Concealed among unruly wilderness are four architectural cabins on stilts, strategically placed to ensure total seclusion while also offering sensational views of the Cornish landscape.

These structures are designed for the adventurous traveller, a challenge to navigate but very comfortable once inside. Alternatively you may choose to opt for a tree tent, which can be set up wherever you choose in the fairytale woodland, or for the Danish Cabin, a whimsical building in the woods.

During the day, the team offer a variety of activities on site including foraging, yoga and beachcombing. Breakfast and meals can be provided but campfire cooking is encouraged.

Kudhva translates to 'hideout', a fitting name for this secluded haven, and provides an extremely memorable Cornish getaway, well worth seeking out.

ST TUDY INN

—

Restaurant & Rooms

St Tudy, Bodmin, PL30 3NN
01208 850 656
sttudyinn.com

Emily Scott is an ambitious and optimistic chef, who took over this inn determined to offer locals and visitors great food and comfortable rooms in a delightful setting. The charming Cornish pub is situated in St Tudy, a quaint village in North Cornwall, and deservedly holds a Michelin Bib Gourmand. After an extensive redecoration, the pub feels cosy and welcoming, with original artworks by Cornish artists including Nicole Heidaripour and worn vintage furniture.

All of Emily's cheffing experience is put to good use in the kitchen, where seasonality and local produce reign. The menu is full of comforting classics with a twist; fish and chips for example is upgraded to the irresistibly tasty Monkfish tails in rosemary focaccia crumb with fries and citrus mayonnaise. The drinks list features a bespoke brew, The Monty Dog Pale Ale, made in collaboration with Harbour Brewing Co, and a one-off Malbec blend from the Civrac winery in Bordeaux.

Those who wish to extend their visit can stay in one of the simple, cosy bedrooms.

RESTAURANT NATHAN OUTLAW

—

Restaurant

6 New Road, Port Isaac, PL29 3SB
01208 880 896
nathan-outlaw.com

A veritable prodigy of the kitchen, Nathan Outlaw worked under Gary Rhodes and Rick Stein before establishing his own reputation, opening the first two-Michelin-star fish restaurant in the UK. It is a clean, stylish dining room in Port Isaac with sharp service and immaculate seafood dishes.

Outlaw's food is blissfully minimalist, he aims 'to take ingredients away from the plate rather than add' which allows the Cornish produce, always cooked to perfection, to shine. The set menu features delights such as Gurnard with Porthilly Sauce, one of Outlaw's most elegant and brilliant recipes.

If you can't secure a table at Restaurant Nathan Outlaw, head to Port Isaac's charming harbour where Nathan has his more relaxed Outlaw's Fish Kitchen, also to Michelin acclaim.

CARN MAR

—

Holiday Home

Cliff Lane, Polzeath, PL27 6UE
latitude50.co.uk

Many fondly think of Cornwall as a second home, somewhere to relax and escape from their everyday life. The Latitude50 properties provide getaways for just this purpose; luxurious and welcoming dwellings along the North Cornwall coast to rent for a weekend minibreak or a longer holiday.

Latitude50 was founded two decades ago and over the years has managed and rented out a wide range of self-catering beachside cottages and waterfront homes to Cornwall visitors.

Carn Mar is one of their most special homes, ideally located on the edge of the beach at Polzeath. This expansive retreat has six bedrooms, a large open-plan kitchen and numerous pristine common spaces for guests to enjoy. But it is the outdoor surroundings that make Carn Mar truly special. It feels wonderful to wake up to panoramic views of the sea, with the vibrant garden to picnic in and even a fire pit for chillier al fresco evenings.

SURFSIDE

—

Restaurant & Bar

On the Beach, Polzeath, PL27 6TB
01208 862 931
surfsidepolzeath.com

Surfside is an exciting venture from London-based mixologist Tristan Stephenson, author of The Curious Bartender and co-founder of Purl and The Whistling Shop bars in London. Surfside has become a local hit, serving fresh food and cocktails at the water's edge in Polzeath. Located on a corner of the beach, the restaurant is only accessible via the sand, which adds to the experience.

Although the venue appears casual from the exterior, inside the offerings are for serious foodies with surf and turf platters and inventive cocktails. Thanks to the isolated location, Surfside feels intimate and exclusive with panoramic sea views adding something special to the meal.

Behind the main restaurant, a buzzy, outdoor rum bar serves tiki cocktails and features live music in the summer months.

PAUL AINSWORTH AT NO. 6

—

Restaurant

6 Middle Street, Padstow, PL28 8AP
01841 532 093
paul-ainsworth.co.uk/number6

Housed within a historic Georgian Townhouse on a quaint Padstow street, Paul Ainsworth at No. 6 is the chef's most prestigious restaurant. The playful and creative dishes showcase Cornwall's finest seasonal ingredients while hinting at his varied culinary influences.

The restaurant has a cosy and relaxed feel, with a private dining room for special occasions. At lunchtime a set menu allows guests to sample his signature flavours at a very reasonable price. Look out for the nostalgic 'A Fairground Tale' dessert, which has received particular recognition and is a favourite on the menu. Next door, Executive Chef John Walton runs Mahé, an intimate cooking school and chef's table for keen foodie visitors.

For more casual cuisine visit the chef's Rojano's in the Square bistro, or The Mariners, a much-loved pub in Rock. Just a few minutes walk away from No. 6, Padstow Townhouse is an eclectic place to stay.

TREVIBBAN MILL

—

Vineyard

Dark Lane, near Padstow, PL27 7SE
01841 541 413
trevibbanmill.com

Situated on the slopes of the Issey Brook near Padstow, Trevibban Mill is one of the newer Cornish wineries but is already producing award-winning wines. Liz and Engin began planting in 2008 with an ambition to produce top quality Cornish wines and ciders. Native sheep graze on the land and their wool is for sale in the vineyard shop. Tours and tastings can be arranged to sample a range of the different wine and cider varieties.

The popular Grand Walking Tour takes place every weekend, an opportunity to learn about viticulture and grape growing in England. Afterwards you'll sample eight wines and enjoy a light lunch, overlooking the grounds.

Surrounded by lush vineyards and orchards, Trevibban Mill has also become a popular venue for weddings and events, and the private lake is perfect for special ceremonies.

THE SCARLET

—

Hotel

Tredragon Road, Mawgan Porth, Newquay, TR8 4DQ
01637 861 800
scarlethotel.co.uk

Perched on the rugged cliff tops overlooking Mawgan Porth, The Scarlet is the ultimate eco retreat. A rare, adults-only establishment in Cornwall, The Scarlet is an instantly calming place in which to spend time. It features fresh contemporary bedrooms, many of which boast private garden terraces or balconies, and an exemplary restaurant with seasonal dishes overseen by Head Chef Mike Francis.

The hotel proudly allows dogs in some rooms for a small fee per night, or if you fancy a bit of exercise on the beach, you can borrow the hotel dog, the ideal walking companion.

Downstairs, the destination spa offers Ayurvedic treatments to nourish body and soul and a soothing Relaxing Room with hanging cocoon pods for post-treatment sleeps. Rest in the outdoor sauna or soak in the clifftop hot tub which offers dramatic views across the Atlantic.

PAVILION

—

Bakery & Café

37 Fore Street, Newquay, TR7 1HD
wearethepavilion.com

A rare export from London, Pavilion opened shop on Fore Street in Newquay in 2017. This hipster café and bakery is much like its original stores in East London, stacked high with its celebrated sourdough bread and full of other appetising baked goods.

The Pavilion story began in Sri Lanka, where founder Rob fell in love with the country's culture, food and community. He returned home with a mission, and set up his first café in Victoria Park in London serving up signature Sri Lankan breakfasts and great speciality coffee and tea.

Pavilion opened several successful bakeries in London before making themselves at home in Newquay. Here you can find flaky pastries, indulgent brunch dishes and freshly baked sourdough bread, either to have in or to take away and enjoy on the beach.

WATERGATE BAY HOTEL

—

Hotel

On The Beach, Watergate Bay, Newquay, TR8 4AA
01637 860 543
watergatebay.co.uk

Watergate Bay Hotel, in North Cornwall, is set on one of the area's most spectacular beaches. With two miles of golden sand and an impressive swell from the Atlantic, it is a popular destination for surfers. Dolphins are often spotted jumping through the azure sea. The hotel has light, laid-back double rooms and family suites with bunkrooms, making it suitable for both romantic getaways and family holidays. The decor is fresh and modern with splashes of colour and seaside artwork that remind guests of their coastal location.

Downstairs, the stylish Swim Club offers an indoor infinity pool and private rooms for spa treatments. Food options are plentiful with four venues onsite including Zacry's for evening meals, casual seaside classics at The Beach Hut, and The Living Space for all-day dining. Watchful Mary is their newest bar; a lovely place to sit with a craft cocktail or speciality coffee while watching the waves lap on the shore.

NANCARROW

—

Farm & Feasts

Zelah, near Truro, TR4 9DQ
01872 487 099
nancarrowfarm.co.uk

The fayres, festivals and feast nights at Nancarrow Farm have become renowned across West Cornwall; popular with locals and visitors, they sell out fast. Primarily a family-run farm, the scenic 100-acre grounds have produced an abundance of high-quality, certified organic meats for over 20 years. For nine generations the farmers, their family and friends have eaten around the kitchen table enjoying hearty home-cooked dishes and their Barn Ale own brew.

With a professional kitchen, larder and butchery onsite, the team welcome guests to memorable events, private cookery workshops, and exciting feast nights. Each month a new menu is designed around the farm's own produce; everything is cooked in a wood-fired oven with live music providing an atmospheric accompaniment.

There are also nine charming en-suite bedrooms and tipis in the orchard for guests to book, if staying over.

DOR & TAN

—

Shop

Unit 1, Treglisson Rural Workshops, Wheal Alfred Road, Hayle, TR27 5JT
01736 447 090
dorandtan.com

The tradition of ceramics is intrinsically linked to the Cornish coast. Dor & Tan is a ceramic design studio and shop close to St Ives, and the small team design, develop and create tableware for all occasions.

The team is led by head ceramicist Sharron who, along with Peter, Matthew and Viola, runs the small but efficient studio. Each handmade piece is created with love and care, with the intention of making something lasting to cherish but to enjoy using everyday. As well as developing their own range for shops across the country, the team design bespoke pieces for restaurants and coffee shops.

Dor & Tan produce a rare example of modern but timeless pottery, which can be used regularly but appreciated for its beauty and design. Visitors can stop by the little shop to see the current collection and also visit the onsite working studio by appointment.

TATE ST IVES

—

Gallery

Porthmeor Beach, St Ives, TR26 1TG
01736 796 226
tate.org.uk

Tate St Ives reopened in Autumn 2017 after an extensive and dramatic refurbishment and expansion.

The famous art gallery is perched on the edge of Porthmeor Beach. Coastal daylight floods into the museum through the large windows and rooflights, illuminating the works and adding a magical glow to the rooms. With the renovation, the gallery space has doubled in size, allowing much more art to be on display.

The gallery's display collection holds important works by modern British artists with a link to this area of Cornwall. You will find significant works by Barbara Hepworth, Peter Lanyon and Sandra Blow, amongst others.

On the top floor, Tate St Ives' café has the best panoramic views in town.

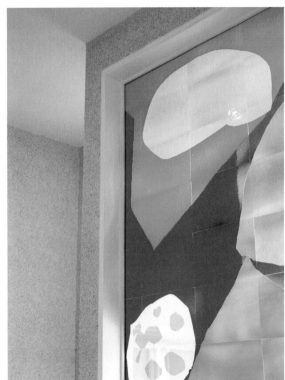

TREVOSE HARBOUR HOUSE

—

Hotel

22 The Warren, St Ives, TR26 2EA
01736 793 267
trevosehouse.co.uk

St Ives is the most popular town to visit in Cornwall, with a beautiful coastline and many cultural highlights. Located in the centre of town, Trevose Harbour House was reopened by Angela and Olivier Noverraz in 2013 after a full restoration. The six stylish bedrooms feel fresh and suit the seaside surroundings.

In the summer months, the suntrap terrace is a lovely place to relax, and in winter the cosy living room has an open fireplace and an honesty bar. Angela and Olivier take pride in the breakfast they provide: a feast of organic continental delights and an array of nourishing hot dishes.

For the best views of the harbour, book the rooftop suite, a glorious bedroom and bathroom decorated with accents of mid-century design while providing every luxury you could need.

BARBARA HEPWORTH MUSEUM
AND SCULPTURE GARDEN

—

Museum

Barnoon Hill, St Ives, TR26 1AD
01736 796 226
tate.org.uk

Nestled among tropical shrubs and exotic flowers stand the solemn sculptures of Barbara Hepworth, Cornwall's leading lady.

The Trewyn Studios appear as if untouched since Hepworth ended her days here in 1975 and the workshop and intimate garden have a quiet, peaceful atmosphere. Sheltered from the fierce coastal winds, it is a fertile oasis, especially in spring when the blossom is out. The garden is particularly enchanting early in the morning before all the tourists arrive.

St Ives has a long history as a home for major artists, potters and sculptors, but Barbara Hepworth was undoubtedly the most prolific and potent.

SANDS & SAMPHIRE
STUDIOS

—

Holiday Apartments

Beach Court, Porthgwidden, St Ives, TR26 1PL
01736 317 740
stives-studios.co.uk

Quietly tucked away on St Ives Island are the stylish Sands and Samphire studios. These beautifully designed apartments are owned and run by Angela and Olivier Noverraz, of Trevose Harbour House.

Spacious yet cosy, the studios each provide a luxurious and private retreat for couples wishing to escape the busy central hub of this popular coastal town. Themed by colour, the rooms are decorated with carefully chosen vintage furniture and artistic details.

Samphire Studio is found on the ground floor with a vibrant green decor inspired by its exotic garden. Upstairs, Sands Studio offers particularly magnificent views of the sea and golden beaches, and the unique furniture echoes the yellow hues. The apartments have all the necessary amenities to ensure you truly find a home away from home.

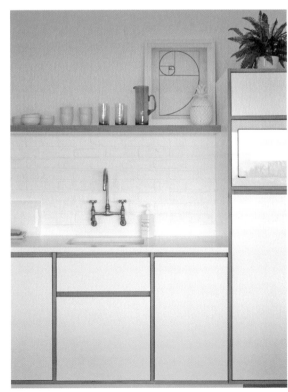

PLUMBLINE

—

Shop

2 Barnoon Hill, St Ives, TR26 1AD
07703 797 060
plumblinestives.co.uk

Plumbline is a discreet design shop well worth seeking out. The small space is perfectly curated - a pristine gallery for stylish shoppers wishing to discover something exceptional.

Deborah, the imaginative owner, handpicks items from a variety of talented artists from all over the country. Plumbline's stock is a stark contrast to the seaside memorabilia that fills the more touristy shops. Jochen Holz, the East London glassblower, has a range of his striking work featured here, alongside elegant ceramics by Sam Hall.

Behind the shop there is a small, good-looking flat for visitors to rent; a design haven for the aesthetically inclined traveller.

PORT OF CALL

—

Shop

9 Market Place, St Ives, TR26 1RZ
01736 796 211
academyandco.com

Port of Call is the third retail space from Kate and James Deseta, a brother and sister team bringing clean aesthetics and a love of design to St Ives.

The carefully displayed homeware items and magazines are sure to induce domestic envy. The shop stocks niche brands - there is organic skincare by Grown Alchemist from Australia, Ondine Ash's ethically-produced patterned cushions and beautiful ceramics from St Ives' own Dor & Tan. Alongside the lifestyle items, there is a selection of pretty house plants and accessories, and you can also stock up on speciality journals and inspiring travel books.

Nearby, their clothing store, Academy & Co, stocks diverse designers like Norse Projects and Ally Capellino, while a third shop, Number 8, focuses on streetwear and trainers.

THE OLD CUSTOM HOUSE

—

Restaurant

Upstairs, Customs House, Wharf Road, St Ives, TR26 1LF
01736 799 943
theoldcustomhouse.co.uk

As one of Cornwall's most popular tourist towns, St Ives has its fair share of chain eateries, especially along the main harbour. Skip the usual suspects and head to The Old Custom House, a dinky restaurant by couple Haley Sugden and Stephen Knowles with a refreshing approach to dining.

It is easy to miss the discreet staircase that leads up to the seven table restaurant, but as soon as you enter you will know you are in the right place as host Haley will welcome you with open arms and a wide smile. Perch at the bar with an apéritif or sit down at a table with enviable views over the famous harbour.

Stephen's menu is Italian inspired, an ever-evolving seasonal selection of tapas-style plates designed for sharing. The Old Custom House is a rare gem in the St Ives food scene and a must if you are staying in town.

ANIMA MUNDI

—

Gallery

Street-an-Pol, St Ives, TR26 2DS
01736 793 121
animamundigallery.com

There are plenty of art galleries in St Ives to peruse, but few that select and present contemporary work as beautifully as Anima Mundi.

The gallery was founded by Joseph Clarke who sought to give a bold platform to local and international artists of promise. The roster boasts renowned names including Tim Shaw RA and Sarah Ball, who gladly fill the pristine walls of the three-tiered exhibition space with their most prominent works.

Over the last 20 years, Anima Mundi has showcased the work of artists in all media; it is a rare luxury for the artists to have such a large space to exhibit their work. The statuesque building on Street-an-Pol is slightly off the tourist track, but worth a wander as the exhibitions are always thought provoking and striking.

YALLAH COFFEE KIOSK

—

Coffee Hatch

Court Arcade, St Ives, TR26 1LF
yallahcoffee.co.uk

Yallah Coffee Roasters has been supplying many of Cornwall's best loved cafés and restaurants ever since they started roasting beans from their barn on Argal Home Farm. Sustainability is at the heart of the business; their single origin beans are very carefully sourced and their roastery is powered by solar energy and heated with biomass.

The Yallah Coffee Kiosk opened in St Ives in July 2018, a welcome addition to the harbour stretch, ideal for picking up a caffeinated treat before a sandy stroll. The little white and green hatch is a quaint takeaway option for coffee obsessives and those who really care about drinking the best speciality coffee. The Yallah team serve flavour-forward coffee, roasted with precision and perfectly poured.

If you are peckish there is always a small range of sweet snacks to choose from to accompany your drink.

LEACH POTTERY

—

Museum

Higher Stennack, St Ives, TR26 2HE
01736 799 703
leachpottery.com

St Ives is a notably artistic area of Britain with a long list of influential painters and potters making their home here. Founded in 1920 by Bernard Leach and Shoji Hamada as a place for potters to train and learn their trade, Leach Pottery is one of the most famous ceramic institutions in the UK.

Today, the pottery continues to operate as a working studio with the museum and gallery offering an insight into its history. The exhibition space presents the work of international and local potters, with occasional residencies from celebrated artists from around the world.

There is also a shop onsite where you can purchase a special piece from the Leach Standard Ware range.

THE GURNARD'S HEAD

—

Pub, Restaurant & Rooms

near Zennor, St Ives, TR26 3DE
01736 796 928
gurnardshead.co.uk

Despite its isolated location in the countryside between St Just and St Ives, The Gurnard's Head is always busy with loyal locals and visiting guests. This welcoming, mustard-yellow pub is a beacon of warmth among the stark green fields, serving hearty but refined food that will satisfy every appetite, but is particularly rewarding after a long coastal walk.

Inside you can opt for a drink at the bar or a full meal in the civilised dining room. Max Wilson has been head chef at the inn since June 2016 and continues to excel with his nurturing and innovative recipes, from classic fish dishes to modern seasonal inventions. The Gurnard's Head is particularly popular for Sunday lunch when they serve a roast that is second to none.

There are also seven bedrooms if you wish to stay. Rooms 1 and 7 have a view of the sea, but some might prefer the vistas of the rugged Cornish countryside.

THE MINACK THEATRE

—

Theatre

Porthcurno, TR19 6JU
01736 810 181
minack.com

Concealed within the scenic cliffs of Porthcurno is the enchanting Minack Theatre. The project was first imagined and built by Rowena Cade, who lived nearby, in Minack House. From 1931, Rowena and her gardener tirelessly moved boulders to create a space for actors to perform and tiered steps to accommodate spectators. The first production, a version of The Tempest, was performed in this curious venue in 1932 and the theatre is still very much in use during the warmer months.

With the turquoise waters lapping at Porthcurno Beach in the background, it is a dramatic and magical setting in which to witness any play. You can also visit during the day, when there is no performance, to view the site and learn about the theatre's history.

LOVETTS

—

Café & Wine Bar

1 The Coombe, Newlyn, Penzance, TR18 5HS
lovetts-newlyn.co.uk

Whether you stop by Lovetts in the morning, at noon or at night, there is always something to make you smile at this tiny, cornershop café and wine bar.

The venue is owned by husband and wife, Rohit and Emma, who work tirelessly to source and serve the finest drinks and snacks for visitors.

Emma is in charge of coffee, which she proudly makes with Origin beans on a gleaming La Marzocco machine. Tempting baked delights are all made locally and include sweet treats from Oona's Cakes. If you are after something savoury, Lovetts' cheese toasties are indulgent and delicious.

In the late afternoon and evening, Rohit pours glasses of specialist wines, carefully sourced from the finest organic and biodynamic vineyards from around the world.

ARTIST RESIDENCE

—

Hotel

20 Chapel Street, Penzance, TR18 4AW
01736 365 664
artistresidence.co.uk

Chapel Street seems a fitting home for the Cornish branch of Artist Residence. This boutique property opened in 2010 as the second hotel in a rapidly growing group.

The Artist Residence hotels are full of flair and personality thanks to the young and entrepreneurial couple behind the business. Justin and Charlie Salisbury originally asked local artists to design and paint the bedrooms at this quaint Penzance hotel in exchange for board, and some of these artistic rooms still remain today.

The hotel now has 22 eclectically decorated bedrooms and a three-bedroom cottage for families or groups. The rooms bring the essence of Penzance indoors, with seaside-inspired artwork, antique furniture and a minibar stocked with Cornish treats. One of the most popular bedrooms is number 17, a small but beautiful room with plenty of natural light and an indulgent roll-top bathtub.

The resident restaurant, The Cornish Barn, serves hearty dishes and there is also a living room bar area for enjoying a drink by the fire.

NO. 56

—

Shop

14 Chapel Street, Penzance, TR18 4AW
01736 366 293
no-56.com

Chapel Street in Penzance is a shopper's paradise with an assortment of unique design and retro outlets. On a sunny afternoon, it is a lovely lane to explore, stopping at each shop to rummage through the vintage trinkets or peruse the desirable objects and garments.

After a career in mens and womenswear design, Carole Elsworth set up No. 56 where she uses her experience to put together a personal collection based on natural materials and simple designs.

The shop has a fine assortment of stationery and homeware, displayed in a fresh minimalist setting. Pick up a bottle of J Herbin violet-scented ink, a couple of beeswax candles or a minimalist ceramic piece by local potter, Rebecca Proctor. Carole is constantly expanding the range to include her own label 'Handworked' alongside her latest favourite finds, from Cornwall and further afield.

While in town, be sure to visit No. 56's second shop, found at 12 Parade Street, which has a similar ethos and focuses on hand-crafted items.

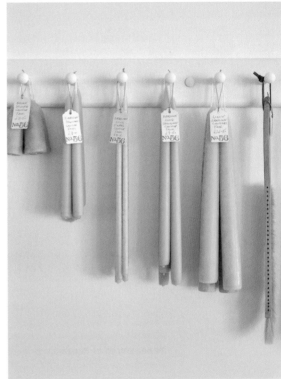

CHAPEL HOUSE

—

Hotel

Chapel Street, Penzance, TR18 4AQ
01736 362 024
chapelhousepz.co.uk

This beautiful, restored townhouse is on the corner of Chapel Street, one of Penzance's most picturesque roads. With views overlooking the sea and St Michael's Mount, it is in an enviable position. Owner Susan Stuart saw an opportunity to renovate and refresh this grand historic building, previously the home of the Penzance Arts Club, offering Penzance visitors a serene and luxurious place to stay.

The boutique hotel has six double bedrooms and two spacious suites to choose from, each is thoughtfully designed with a mix of antique pieces and modern amenities. Reclaimed 1930s office lamps frame the bespoke beds, and a mini iPad in each room allows you to video call for room service should you need it. Room 2 is particularly beautiful with an Ashton & Bentley bathtub and lots of natural light. Wherever possible, Susan supports local makers and suppliers; toiletries are sourced from Penzance beauty brand, Pure Nuff Stuff, and the artwork on the walls is loaned from Newlyn School of Art.

Susan's delicious breakfasts and dinners are enjoyed in the communal dining room and in the next-door boot room you can find wellies for muddy walks and blankets to borrow on chillier days.

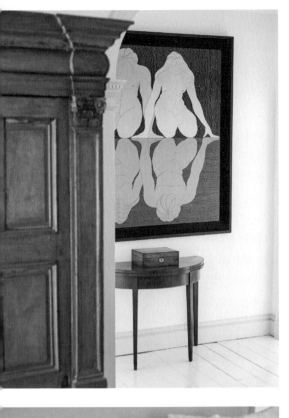

TOTTI

—

Restaurant

41 Market Jew Street, Penzance, TR18 2HX
07754 519 958

Penzance continues to thrive with excellent restaurant openings, from fine dining to cheap eats. Totti is a friendly, local pizza place, on the corner of Market Jew Street.

The eatery is sparse but stylish, with a turquoise theme throughout the décor and pretty original stained glass windows above the door. The name Totti is inspired by the owner's love of football and a bright blue Italian football shirt emblazoned with the Italian player's name hangs significantly on the wall.

The Neapolitan style pizza is fresh and tasty, utilising the best locally grown ingredients. Totti have also become known for their ideal lunch option - the Panuozzo, a pizza sandwich - and have a great selection of traditional Sicilian cannoli if you fancy something sweet.

Eat in - there are a limited number of bar stools - or buy your pizza to take away.

JUBILEE POOL

—

Lido & Café

Battery Road, Penzance, TR18 4FF
01736 369 224
jubileepool.co.uk

Recently restored to its former glory, Jubilee Pool is once again the pride of Penzance. It was originally designed by Captain F. Latham in the early 1930s and the unique Art Deco shape is inspired by a seagull landing on the water. Where possible, original details have been kept, notably the welcoming 'Bathing Pool' sign and the cubist influenced changing rooms.

Surprisingly, Jubilee is one of the only remaining saltwater tidal pools left in Europe. The main pool is suitable for all swimmers, while a smaller pool accommodates young children. A new geothermal pool provides warmer waters for winter swims.

A relaxed café at the poolside is a welcome addition for athletic visitors needing sustenance or a refreshing drink. The lido is a glorious spot for summer swims or family picnics, and the brilliant blue pools are a beautiful addition to the Penzance coast.

TREMENHEERE SCULPTURE GARDENS

—

Gallery & Gardens

near Gulval, Penzance, TR20 8YL
01736 448 089
tremenheere.co.uk

This vast and verdant garden in Penzance is definitely not just for art enthusiasts; the route through the epic plants and trees will transport you from the moment you step inside. A short drive from the town, Tremenheere is a dramatic setting for impressive sculptural works both permanent and temporary. The unique positioning and climate allow exotic plants and flowers to flourish, creating a tropical world. From the top of the hill there are magical vistas of St Michael's Mount and the coastline.

Renowned artists such as Richard Long, Peter Randall-Page and Tim Shaw have interacted with the landscape to create specific works that complement the setting, but James Turrell's Skyspace (Tewlwolow Kernow) is perhaps the most mesmerising work, an oval space showing the ever-changing sky. In wetter weather, the two-storey timber art gallery is a lovely indoor space, featuring some of the finest artists in West Cornwall.

After exploring the gardens, visit Tremenheere Kitchen for wholesome food and the shop, Artisan, for a small selection of thoughtful gifts. Tremenheere also has a plant nursery that sells a wide range of interesting succulents.

NEW YARD

—

Restaurant

Trelowarren, Mawgan, Helston, TR12 6AF
01326 221 595
newyardrestaurant.co.uk

Those who know about New Yard visit regularly, raving about the wholesome food and lovely laid-back atmosphere.

The restaurant is found in the historic old stableyard deep within Trelowarren Estate, close to the Lizard, which is the southernmost tip of Cornwall. The rugged natural gardens of Trelowarren are alluring and unspoilt, and it would be easy to get lost wandering around the picturesque grounds.

New Yard is spacious and welcoming with rustic tables and a roaring fire in the winter. The chefs hail from some of the county's finest restaurants, and whip up seasonal and fresh dishes with pride and enthusiasm. The food is unfussy and delicious, with an emphasis on local fish. In the summer months there is also a pizzeria for homemade, wood-fired pizzas.

POTAGER GARDEN

—

Café

High Cross, Constantine, Falmouth, TR11 5RF
01326 341 258
potagergarden.org

Nestled in the enchanting Constantine countryside, Potager Garden is a lovely place to spend time, indulging in a healthy vegetarian feast in the greenhouse or a refreshing drink in the sunshine outside. This daytime café was an abandoned plant nursery before it was transformed into a picturesque haven for eating and relaxing. The chefs, led by Daisy Hillier, use organic produce from the gardens to create vibrant and delicious recipes.

Six studios onsite are used by resident artists and frequent Open Studio days allow the public to view the work for free. The surrounding gardens are constantly evolving, with a wealth of beautiful flowers, so it is always a rewarding place to visit.

On occasion, Potager Garden also hosts evening meals, from lively banquets to fine dining feasts.

THE SANDY DUCK

—

Bed & Breakfast

12 Pennance Road, Falmouth, TR11 4EA
01326 311 427
thesandyduck.co.uk

The Sandy Duck, just outside Falmouth, is a relaxing and calm place to stay. This stylish, boutique B&B has eight bedrooms and is decorated in pale shades with a Scandinavian aesthetic in mind. The contemporary design is interspersed with unique antique furniture and special family mementos and artwork.

Owner-manager Freyja previously spent time aboard luxury yachts cooking and crewing before arriving in Cornwall to open The Sandy Duck. She poured her time and care into transforming this Edwardian townhouse into a lovely minibreak retreat.

Many of the rooms offer sea views, while others feature indulgent freestanding bathtubs. Breakfast is served in the airy dining room downstairs where Freyja cooks up tempting delights.

TORO

—

Shop

Old Brewery Yard, High Street, Falmouth, TR11 2BY
toro-studio.com

Falmouth is a town of creatives and has spawned many inventive projects and businesses. Toro is found in the Old Brewery Yard, among a number of artistic boutiques - it is a small and lush botanical studio crowded with whimsical hanging plants and shelves of cacti. The plants look at home on the shop's attractive wood furniture, some of which is created by local designer, Heather Scott.

Toro owner, Tor Harrison, champions plants for indoor spaces and believes plants have the power to change the dynamics of a space, adding character while lifting the mood. She is also passionate about supporting artisan makers and you can find unique pieces by British ceramicists such as Isatu Hyde, Tim Lake and Sam Marks in her shop.

Pick a plant or choose from Toro's selection of Bashō natural skincare, made locally from organic botanicals. To keep your succulents healthy, ask Tor for advice on how to water and nurture them.

ESPRESSINI

—

Café

39 Killigrew Street, Falmouth, TR11 3PW
espressini.co.uk

There are more and more promising independent coffee shops in Cornwall; Espressini on Killigrew Street in Falmouth is one of the best. This characterful venue serves a bespoke selection of single-farm beans sourced and roasted by Yallah Coffee, selected specially for them from growers around the world. Inside, the café is cosy and familiar with mismatched antique furniture, and the chatter is accompanied by a thoughtful playlist.

The coffee is bold in flavour and served to your preference. Brunch is particularly popular, with a menu of tempting and indulgent dishes displaying a wide range of influences from world cuisines.

Nearby, on Falmouth Harbour, is Dulce, the smaller sibling of Espressini which, as well as offering freshly brewed coffee, sells equipment to help you make the perfect cup at home.

BOTANICAL ATELIER

—

Shop

19a Arwenack Street, Falmouth, TR11 3JA
botanicalatelier.co.uk

You could spend hours poring over every object in Botanical Atelier, a nature inspired shop on Falmouth's Arwenack Street. Neatly tucked into the centre of town, it is a welcome break from the mainstream chains and big brands.

Owner Sarah Jane Humphrey is a botanical illustrator and opened the shop in November 2018. The whimsical boutique was intended as a calm space for workshops, as well as a place to sell her artworks alongside handpicked gifts and items that inspire her.

Sarah's work is delicate and charming, showing her scientific approach to nature. The small shop is beautifully arranged, with fig and avocado drawings on the walls complemented by tempting lifestyle books, trinkets and drawing materials.

BEACON COFFEE

—

Coffee Shop

28a High Street, Falmouth, TR11 2AD
beaconcoffee.co.uk

The speciality coffee movement is gathering momentum in Cornwall, and Falmouth is benefitting more than most.

Beacon Coffee was opened in early 2018 by a team of expert baristas who hail from longstanding coffee house Espressini. The modern, Scandi-inspired space is an inviting place to catch up with friends or to quietly work, while being fuelled by expertly sourced and poured coffee.

Owners Sam and Alex pride themselves on offering a menu of unique and unusual brews and pours, developing the latest trends and investigating alternative methods of making and drinking coffee. They use a constantly rotating selection of beans, including Old Spike and Colonna.

Opt for the One & One, a single espresso and a one-shot flat white, allowing you to taste and appreciate one of the their espressos on offer in two different ways.

THE SEAFOOD BAR

—

Tap Room & Restaurant

4 Quay Street, Falmouth, TR11 3HH
01326 712 132
verdantbrewing.co

The craft beer scene is growing rapidly in Cornwall and there are now a number of breweries making great local products. Verdant Brewing Co was founded in 2014 in Falmouth by friends Adam and James, with Rich joining them a few years later. The trio had an aim to create unfiltered, vegan, hoppy craft beer.

The Verdant family's brewhouse is just outside Falmouth. Their Seafood Bar, off the Falmouth high street, serves a long list of their fine beers alongside inventive recipes showcasing fresh local seafood. The chefs offer a select menu of vibrant fish dishes, which pair brilliantly with the beers. You can expect delights like lobster and crayfish roll, seasonal ceviche and moreish fried seafood balls.

From the eight taps at the bar, four serve core range classics, while the other four provide ever-changing seasonal options. Lightbulb is a favourite, a very pale ale with savoury notes and a hint of citrus.

THE WAREHOUSE,
ORIGIN COFFEE ROASTERS

—

Coffee Shop

Commercial Road, Penryn, TR10 8AE
01326 617 100
origincoffee.co.uk

Founded by Tom Sobey in 2004, Origin specialise in sourcing and roasting exceptional coffee. The company was founded in Cornwall and their Roastery and Training Lab in Helston is available for tours, with prior booking.

In 2013, Origin opened their first coffee shop at Harbour Head in Porthleven, supplying locals with high quality coffee and a relaxed, contemporary space with seaside views.

As their reputation grew so did the family of coffee shops. In 2018, The Warehouse burst onto the sleepy Penryn scene, an airy and stylish space to enjoy a superior coffee and the best brunch in town. The hearty and healthy menu reflects quality and provenance, perfectly complementing their single-origin coffees.

Origin also have shops across London; in Shoreditch, Southwark and at The British Library.

THE HIDDEN HUT

—

Café & Feasts

Porthcurnick Beach, Portscatho, TR2 5EW
hiddenhut.co.uk

Simon Stallard has popularised the notion of 'feasts' in Cornwall and his al fresco events have become a phenomenal sell-out success.

By day, The Hidden Hut is an unassuming wooden shed, perched on the edge of the Roseland Peninsula, on a National Trust coastal path. It is here that Simon and his team serve up tasty fare, from homemade Cornish pasties to hot crab soup, which guests enjoy on the sharing tables. It is blissfully relaxed and nostalgic, just a few steps up from the beach.

The highly anticipated feasts take place sporadically on the same plot of land. Guests bring their own plates, cutlery and drinks and gorge on whatever the team are cooking up, such as lobsters on the BBQs or a giant seafood paella. It is a joyful experience and the reasonably priced tickets sell out in seconds.

Simon and his wife have also opened Tatams in the town of Portscatho, a short walk from The Hidden Hut. On a sunny day there is nothing better than sipping a Tatams coffee with the rippling sea in the distance.

FITZROY

—

Restaurant

2 Fore Street, Fowey, PL23 1AQ
01726 932 934
fitzroycornwall.com

Fitzroy has put Fowey back on the map as a Cornwall food destination. The venue comes from the team behind London eateries Primeur, Westerns Laundry and Jolene, and the concept is not dissimilar - a relaxed menu of appetising, seasonal, small plates intended to be shared by the table.

Chef and co-owner David Gingell hails from Cornwall and his pride and love for the county is evident in every detail at Fitzroy. The furniture is made by local craftsmen, Able Provisions, and adds a unique character to the room. Upstairs, a private dining room is ideal for intimate events, but it is in the main space that you feel the energy and expertise from everyone involved in this project.

Indulge with a glass of carefully chosen wine, and a few plates of whatever the staff recommend.

ISLES OF SCILLY

—

Islands

Those in the know about British travel take an annual pilgrimage to the Isles of Scilly. Of the 1500 or so islands in the archipelago, only five are inhabited. After a short flight or boat journey from the mainland to St Mary's, the other islands are accessible by water taxi just ten minutes or less apart. The serene waters and warm climate provide an idyllic retreat for visitors and a safe, quiet lifestyle for the islanders.

Choose an island destination dependent on what you desire from a holiday: Tresco for luxurious bliss, Bryher for a rugged remote escape or St Agnes for an isolated artistic retreat. Accommodation varies from campsites to rented sea-view cottages, or for something extra special book in to Hell Bay Hotel. Local restaurants celebrate the produce from the surrounding ocean and communal feasting at The Crab Shack is not to be missed.

There are plenty of sea-based activities to enjoy and on land the Tresco Abbey Garden is the most visited attraction. With hundreds of exotic plants, flowers and trees carefully selected from all over the world and immaculately nurtured, it is quite a spectacle, especially when the sun shines.

SIMON STALLARD
—
CHEF/OWNER - THE HIDDEN HUT & TATAMS

Simon Stallard set up The Hidden Hut in 2011. Perched on a cliff overlooking the remote Porthcurnick Beach, the outdoor restaurant has no road access and is completely off grid. As well as daily dishes, Simon cooks up atmospheric open-air feasts for diners throughout the year. In the summer seasons tickets sell out within minutes of release, making it the one of the hottest culinary tickets in the UK. Simon's cooking techniques have become iconic in Cornwall - from fire pits in the sand to wind-chime fish smokers and wood-fired rotisseries. Simon also owns Tatams, a relaxed café and tavern serving coffee and snacks in the day, and wood-fired pizzas and grilled meats at night.

What's your earliest memory of food, was it an important part of your childhood?
My grandparents lived an incredibly low impact lifestyle with an apple orchard and a full allotment patch. Growing up with them just down the road gave me great knowledge of fresh ingredients. Big long lunches and family gatherings certainly helped sculpt my love of communal dining and my desire to get lots of people around a table.

Was a career in the kitchen an obvious and easy choice for you?
It just felt like the right path for me to tread. I finished school on the Friday and started my first job as a trainee chef on the Monday.

You aren't originally from Cornwall. What was your connection to the county and why did you choose to open your first venture here, rather than anywhere else?
My first visit to Cornwall was when I was offered a chef position on the Roseland peninsula in 2007. I instantly fell in love with this incredible county and I met my partner, Jem, not long after arriving. She grew up in Portscatho so the Hidden Hut beach was really familiar to her. For me, the quality of the produce mixed with the intensity of the seasons and slow pace of life made this area perfect for the work-life balance I craved. There's nowhere else I can imagine living these days, especially now we have the boys.

The setting for The Hidden Hut is obviously unique, but what about it particularly caught your eye?
The hut just sat perched on the unspoilt cove, what's not to like? When I moved to Cornwall it was obvious that visitors and locals alike loved the beach and for me the thought of combining wholesome seasonal food in this environment felt right.

How do you define your style of cooking?
I'm normally outdoors on the grill. My style is formed from the wood we use for fuel to the produce we source on our doorstep. 'Hyper-local, wood fired' perhaps sums it up.

What are your favourite ingredients to cook with and why?
Shellfish, the location of the hut lends itself amazingly to the bay's shellfish. Scallops cooked in the coals straight from the boat - that takes some beating.

Are there any Cornish ingredients or suppliers you're most proud of?
I love the Cornish saffron that's grown 200 yards up the road. We're extremely fortunate we have our beef in the fields above the hut and enjoy a great relationship with local farmers and fishermen. We're just lucky to be part of this close-knit community.

Your feasts sell out in seconds... can you tell us a bit about them?

The feast nights started in 2011 and have continued to capture people's desires to eat together outdoors. They are a celebration of a few seasonal ingredients carefully put together to create a wholesome supper. The best bit comes from the guests. They bring their own plates, cutlery and booze and are always in good spirits. The feasts are a highlight for us, we're just sorry we can't fit everyone in.

What do you think makes the perfect al fresco meal?

Matching the food to the weather; one of the biggest things to take into account is wind speed and air temperature. We always allow ourselves room to adapt a feast - a hot, restorative plate if it's cold, an uplifting, vibrant dish if it's warm.

What do you want people to feel while experiencing one of your feasts?

I want them to feel it's their night. I love the idea that everyone comes to a feast with a bit of excitement up their sleeve.

As well as The Hidden Hut, you also own Tatams... how does the food differ there?

Tatams is on the next cove along in Portscatho. When The Hidden Hut closes at the end of October we all head over there. The vibe follows all our feast values with BYO etc. It's a great venue where guests order their food, grab a seat indoors or throw blanket on the beach and make the night their own. It's open all year round - with pizzas in the summer and a wood-fired grill in the winter.

You also do lots of pop-ups and events, is there one that particularly stands out?

I'm always on the hunt for interesting places to cook. I see a pop-up event as a great way to try something new and explore. Recently I cooked with Hoste London, in between the vines of London's only vineyard as a collaboration with the super talented host and stylist, Laura Jackson. It's great when a collaboration allows different skills and passions to blend and create something really magical.

How have you seen the food scene in Cornwall change in the last few years?

It continues to get better year on year. We were the only place doing ticketed feast nights when we started out 8 years ago, but it's become a big thing here now. It's fantastic to see, as it's a great way to dine.

Are there any up and coming chefs or restaurants in Cornwall that you're particularly excited about?

Howard Sellers from Bango Kitchen would be my pick at the moment. He's an incredible young chef making massive moves in the up-and-coming area of Penryn. His honest flavours and highly-dressed street food packs a punch.

What's your most unforgettable meal or dish?

I've enjoyed some really beautiful meals. Stand out ones include the Noma staff party and Tetsuya's private dining room. However I think my most memorable was when I was taken to a cement factory in northern Spain. You were lucky if you got a stool to sit on, but the food was just so delicious. Simple, honest, affordable and delicious; inclusive not exclusive.

If you could eat in one restaurant in the world, which would it be?

I have a huge love of wood fired food so it would be a toss up. I've not been to either, but Asador Extebarri or Restaurant Niklas Ekstedt in Sweden.

Who is your greatest inspiration - in work and in life?

Without a doubt my Dad. He's the most unassuming, kind, generous man. He worked day and night to keep our family cogs oiled and gave us the drive and desire to do well and do right.

And finally... if you were on a desert island and only allowed three ingredients, what would you take?

Salt, olive oil and some seasoned wood.

DARREN LITTLE

—

HEAD GARDENER - ST MICHAEL'S MOUNT

Darren Little is the Head Gardener on St Michael's Mount in Cornwall. He was brought up on the Mount from birth and started a career in Horticulture at the age of 16. After moving off the island to further his career in gardening and complete formal qualifications, he gained further experience working at a number of gardens and nurseries in the UK. In 2000, Darren was invited by the 4th Lord St Levan to return to the Mount as a gardener and to live back on the island. He has since been made Head Gardener and is responsible for maintaining all the gardens on the Mount.

What was it like growing up on St Michael's Mount?

Growing up on St Michael's Mount is an experience that I look back on with great fondness. As a child we had the run of the island and could explore the rocky outcrops, climb the trees and make dens in the woods. Swimming and fishing were also regular activities due to the surrounding water.

What's your first memory of the Mount?

My first memory was the filming for Dracula in 1979 when I was four. I remember dressing up in old, dirty clothes, covered in coal soot. I was in the tram yard throwing coal into the tram while they were filming, then we all jumped into an old car where they drove us across the causeway and through the lodge gates heading up towards the castle.

Did the plants and gardens play an important part in your early life?

When I was nine, I had my own allotment in the back garden where I grew salad and vegetables for my own use. This is around the time when I began to really enjoy gardening.

You left the island in your late teens, what brought you back?

I left the island to pursue my career in horticulture. I worked at a couple of gardens and nurseries and continued my horticulture development at college. When I was offered a live-in position as a gardener on St Michael's Mount, I jumped at the chance to return to my roots. Having been recently married and keen to start a family, we felt it was the perfect place to be.

What's in your daily routine?

Every day is different, but each day starts with us taking it in turns to walk around the gardens to check for anything that requires attention. I always make sure all the grass is cut before the castle opens to keep the noise to a minimum. It's also a great time for me to enjoy and admire the gardens before they get busy in the daytime.

What's the most challenging part of your role?

The most challenging part of the gardens for us is working at height. A cliff face flanks our gardens so we have to maintain the cliffs by abseiling from the side of the castle. All the garden waste is then lowered down into the gardens from where we carry it down to the bottom so that it can be disposed of correctly. It helps keep us fit as there's a lot of going up and down!

Tell us what makes the climate so special?

The climate is helped by the mild Gulf Stream. It provides warmth so frosts are a rarity and the rocks act as a huge radiator, absorbing heat during the day and radiating heat at night to create a microclimate for the many exotic plants. The gardens face the sun throughout the day and get additional reflected light off the sea. Given the conditions in the winter, with the sea pounding the shores and the salty winds blowing across the gardens, it's amazing that the lush gardens prosper.

Have you discovered or found anything surprising while working on the mount?
In 2009, I unearthed a bronze age Hoard on the North Westerly side of the Mount. I initially discovered a small axe head under some rocks and later discovered a total of 49 artefacts, including blade fragments, a buckle, a chape and various ingot fragments. The finds were sent to the Royal Albert Memorial Museum for x-rays, cleaning, and inspection. It was then verified by the British Museum that the artefacts dated from the late Bronze Age, making them around 3,000 years old.

What do you want someone to feel while visiting the gardens on St Michael's Mount?
I want people to feel an element of surprise. With every corner you turn there is something different flowering. The climate also allows us to grow rare and unusual plants that most people wouldn't dream of growing in their gardens, like Aloe polyphyllas and Agave albopilosa.

Do you have a favourite plant or tree on St Michael's Mount?
In 2003, I planted a Juglans (walnut tree) in celebration of the birth of my son Luke. The tree is now about 10ft tall and produces lots of walnuts.

And in terms of the landscape, do you have a favourite place or view?
I love standing at the eastern pill box looking up to the castle with the gardens in the foreground. Every day I try to stop and look up through the gardens to the castle as the view is always different, from the flowering plants, to the cloud formations above the castle.

If you could add one plant to the garden, what would it be?
I have always wondered whether the climate on the Mount would allow us to grow an Ananas comosus (pineapple plant). I'm considering planting one next to a Puya Coerulea as the contrast of the pineapples with the silvery leaves of the puya would be great... watch this space!

What's the best thing about living and working on the Mount?
The best thing is being part of the living community. The residents include gardeners, boatmen, maintenance and castle staff. We all pull together when help is required, from preparing the Mount for storms, to helping to get boats out of the harbour. During the evenings, when the public have gone, we have the island to ourselves and often relax with a communal BBQ on the harbour front.

What is your favourite part of Cornwall and why?
I love walking around the cliffs at the far west of Cornwall; Porthcurno, Porthgwarra, Lands End and all the way to Zennor. You can walk for miles admiring the views and the jagged cliffs. The scenery changes around every corner, from looking out to sea to clambering down to small beaches below. Just remember to take a waterproof with you due to our Cornish mizzle.

If you could recommend one other garden in Cornwall, which would it be and why?
To me it would be Trebah gardens, a great tropical valley garden with a stunning backdrop over the Helford River.

How would you describe Cornwall in three words?
Inspiring, fascinating and calming.

Do you have a secret or hidden part of Cornwall that you can tell us about?
I do, and I am still going to keep it a secret!

If you could visit one garden in the world, which would it be?
Kirstenbosch National Botanical Garden in Cape Town, South Africa.

FURTHER IDEAS

—

STRONG ADOLFOS
Speciality coffee shop serving brunch and lunch
from their café in the Hawksfield creative hub.
Hawksfield, Wadebridge, near Padstow, PL27 7LR
01208 816 949
strongadolfos.com

PADSTOW BREWING CO.
Tasting room for the independent microbrewery that
produces a range of artisan beers and ciders.
6 Broad Street, Padstow, PL28 8BS
01841 522 110
padstowbrewing.co.uk

PRAWN ON THE LAWN
Boutique fishmonger and seafood bar, with
24 seats and a menu that changes daily.
11 Duke Street, Padstow, PL28 8AB
01841 532 223
prawnonthelawn.com

THE SORTING OFFICE
Quirky coffee shop in charming St Agnes,
serving baked treats in a cosy setting.
Churchtown, St Agnes, TR5 0ZN
07807 324 088

SCHOONERS
Casual beachfront eatery and bar serving
sharing plates and craft beer with a view.
The Quay, Trevaunance Cove, St Agnes, TR5 0RU
01872 553 149
schoonerscornwall.com

FINISTERRE
Cornish clothing brand making functional and
sustainable garments for outdoor adventures.
Wheal Kitty Workshops, St Agnes, TR5 0RD
01872 554 820
finisterre.com

CANTEEN
Food outlet with a cause and the permanent home
for Cornish catering company Woodfired Canteen.
9 Wheal Kitty Workshops, St Agnes, TR5 0RD
canteencornwall.com

OPEN
Modern and minimalist surfboard factory and store
with a range of handcrafted boards and a small café.
Wheal Kitty Workshops, St Agnes, TR5 0RD
01872 553 918
open.surf

ST IVES BAKERY
Neighbourhood bakery producing decadent sweet
treats, rustic loaves and hand-crimped pasties.
Corner of Fore Street and The Digey, St Ives, TR26 1HR
01736 798 888

THE TOLCARNE INN
Characterful historic pub headed up by chef Ben Tunnicliffe,
showcasing fresh seafood from Newlyn fish market.
9 Tolcarne Terrace, Newlyn, Penzance, TR18 5PR
01736 363 074
tolcarneinn.co.uk

JELBERTS
Traditional ice-cream maker famously serving only one
flavour: vanilla with clotted cream in an old-school cone.
9 New Road, Newlyn,
Penzance, TR18 5PZ

THE EXCHANGE
Contemporary art space in a former telephone exchange,
offering a varied exhibition programme.
Princes Street, Penzance, TR18 2NL
01736 363 715
newlynartgallery.co.uk

THE SHORE
Occupying the Old Buttery, chef Bruce Rennie presents
a refined and flavoursome seafood tasting menu.
13/14 Alverton Street, Penzance, TR18 2QP
01736 362 444
theshorerestaurant.uk

CAST
Cultural charity and centre housing an exhibition
space, artist studios and a lively café.
3 Penrose Road, Helston, TR13 8TP
c-a-s-t.org.uk

KESTLE BARTON
Visionary, multi-purpose creative space
hidden in the Helston countryside.
Manaccan, Helston, TR12 6HU
01326 231 811
kestlebarton.co.uk

STAR & GARTER
Maritime pub at the top of Falmouth's high street
with hearty food and three apartments to rent.
52 High Street, Falmouth, TR11 2AF
01326 316 663
starandgarter.squarespace.com

HIGHCLIFFE
Reasonably-priced, boutique B&B
with eight uniquely designed rooms.
22 Melvill Road, Falmouth, TR11 4AR
01326 314 466
highcliffefalmouth.com

HOTEL TRESANTON
The original design-conscious, Cornish hotel, owned
and designed by the illustrious Olga Polizzi.
27 Lower Castle Road, St Mawes, TR2 5DR
01326 270 055
tresanton.com

TREGOTHNAN
Makers of fine English tea with magnificent gardens;
visit for a guided tour and afternoon tea.
The Woodyard, Tresillian, Truro, TR2 4AJ
01872 520 000
tregothnan.co.uk

DRIFTWOOD
Fresh seaside hotel perched on the dramatic Portscatho coast,
with a prestigious restaurant.
Rosevine, Portscatho, TR2 5EW
01872 580 644
driftwoodhotel.co.uk

WEEKEND JOURNALS

Editor: Milly Kenny-Ryder
thoroughlymodernmilly.com

Designer: Simon Lovell

Photographer: Gabriel Kenny-Ryder
gabrielkennyryder.com

All venues have been visited personally.

In loving memory of John Jesse who provided much creative inspiration to us all.

First Edition published in the United Kingdom in 2016.
Second Edition published in the United Kingdom in 2018.
Third Edition published in the United Kingdom in 2019.

Copyright Information: p. 45 - BOTTOM LEFT: Ella Frears and Ben Sanderson *The Six Pillars of Modernism (detail)* 2017 © Ella Frears and Ben Sanderson; p. 49 - Barbara Hepworth *Spring* 1966 Tate © Bowness; p. 50 - Barbara Hepworth Museum and Sculpture Garden © Bowness; p. 51 - TOP LEFT: Barbara Hepworth *Landscape Sculpture* 1944 Tate (left) and *Idol* 1955-6 (right) Private Collection © Bowness - TOP RIGHT: Barbara Hepworth *Reclining Figures (St Rémy)* 1958 © Bowness - BOTTOM: Interior of Barbara Hepworth Museum with *Sculpture with Colour (Deep Blue and Red)* 1940 Tate © Bowness

Printed in the UK by Taylor Brothers Ltd. using vegetable-based ink, on FSC approved recyclable, uncoated paper.

ISBN: 978-1-9998591-5-2

hello@weekendjournals.co.uk
weekendjournals.co.uk